"12 Steps to Success: Real-Life Stories of Manifestation and Transformation"

Digby R. Kerr

Published by Digby R. Kerr, 2024.

"12 STEPS TO SUCCESS: REAL-LIFE STORIES OF MANIFESTATION AND TRANSFORMATION"

First edition. September 1, 2024.

Copyright © 2024 Digby R. Kerr.

ISBN: 979-8227667465

Written by Digby R. Kerr.

Also by Digby R. Kerr

The Ripple Effect

The Ripple Effect: "A Fable About Embracing Change and Thriving in Uncertainty"

The Ripple Effect: "A Fable About Embracing Change and Thriving in Uncertainty"

Standalone

The Universal Code: Unlocking the Secrets of Happiness, Wealth, and Health

Mastering LinkedIn: A Comprehensive Guide to Building Your Profile, Growing Your Audience, and Leveraging Business Opportunities

The Universal Code: Unlocking the Secrets of Happiness, Wealth, and Health

Cross-Border Trade Compliance: Navigating the Global Marketplace

Report on Trends and Challenges in Logistics Hiring

"12 Steps to Success: Real-Life Stories of Manifestation and Transformation"

This book is dedicated to my very special close friends, family, spirit guides, and Angels who have stood by me through thick and thin on this journey. I couldn't have done it without you all. A heartfelt thanks to two extraordinary people: my dear friend and brother, Desmond Sparks, whose unwavering support has been a beacon in times of trouble, and my lifelong friend and brother, Sean Ruane, whose presence and encouragement made this book a reality.

"12 Steps to Success:
Real-Life Stories of
Manifestation and
Transformation"
Building Wealth, Health and Abundance
by Digby R. Kerr

"12 Steps to Success: Real-Life Stories of Manifestation and Transformation"

'12 Steps to Success: Real-Life Stories of Manifestation and Transformation'" serves as a comprehensive guide for readers eager to harness the principles of the Law of Attraction to achieve their goals. This book is structured around twelve transformative steps, each designed to facilitate a deep understanding of manifestation and provide actionable insights. The outline will highlight key themes, practical exercises, and real-life success stories that illustrate the effectiveness of these principles. Readers will be empowered to embark on their own journey toward health, wealth, and overall success.

The first few sections of the book focus on visualization techniques that are essential for effective manifestation. Readers will learn how to create vivid mental images of their desired outcomes, tapping into the power of their imagination to attract what they want in life. Practical exercises will accompany these concepts, allowing readers to practice visualization daily. The importance of overcoming limiting beliefs will also be explored, as these beliefs often act as barriers to success. Through guided activities and reflective prompts, readers will identify and challenge their limiting thoughts, laying the groundwork for a more abundant mindset.

Daily affirmations play a pivotal role in attracting abundance, and this book emphasizes their transformative impact. Each chapter will include examples of powerful affirmations that readers can incorporate into their daily routines. By repeating these affirmations, individuals can reprogram their subconscious minds and align their thoughts with their desired outcomes. This section will provide a detailed exploration of how affirmations work, along with practical tips for crafting personalized affirmations that resonate with each reader's specific goals.

Gratitude is another crucial theme in the journey of manifestation. The book will delve into the role of gratitude in enhancing attraction, encouraging readers to cultivate a grateful mindset as a way to attract more positivity into their lives. This section will include exercises to help readers develop a gratitude practice, along with real-life stories of individuals who have experienced significant shifts in their lives through gratitude. The integration of meditation practices will also be discussed, providing readers with techniques to align their energy with universal laws and enhance their manifestation efforts.

Finally, the book will culminate in a collection of success stories that showcase the real-life applications of the twelve steps outlined throughout the text. These narratives will serve as inspiration and motivation for readers, illustrating how ordinary individuals have achieved extraordinary outcomes by applying the principles of the Law of Attraction. The outline will also emphasize the importance of emotional alignment in manifestation, guiding readers in understanding how their feelings play a crucial role in attracting their desires. With this structured approach, "12 Steps to Success" aims to equip readers with the knowledge and tools needed to start their manifestation journey today.

Chapter 1: Understanding Manifestation

The Concept of Manifestation

The concept of manifestation is fundamentally rooted in the belief that our thoughts and feelings can shape our reality. At its core, manifestation is the process of bringing our desires into physical form through focused intention, visualization, and alignment with universal laws. This idea aligns closely with the Law of Attraction, which posits that like attracts like, meaning that positive thoughts and emotions will attract positive outcomes. Understanding manifestation requires recognizing the interplay between our mental state, emotional alignment, and the actions we take in our lives.

Visualization techniques are an essential tool in the manifestation process. By creating vivid mental images of our goals and desires, we can effectively communicate our intentions to the universe. This practice not only enhances clarity about what we truly want but also stimulates our emotional connection to those desires. Engaging in regular visualization can increase motivation and inspire actions aligned with our goals, making it a powerful practice for anyone looking to manifest change in their lives.

Overcoming limiting beliefs is another critical aspect of manifestation. Many individuals hold subconscious beliefs that hinder their ability to attract what they desire. These beliefs often stem from past experiences, societal conditioning, or self-doubt. Identifying and reframing these limiting thoughts is essential for successful manifestation. By actively challenging negative beliefs and replacing them with empowering affirmations, individuals can shift their mindset and open themselves to new possibilities. This process not only enhances the effectiveness of the Law of Attraction but also fosters a greater sense of self-worth and confidence.

Daily affirmations play a vital role in attracting abundance and success. By repeating positive statements that reflect our goals and aspirations, we can rewire our subconscious mind to align with our desires. Affirmations serve as a reminder of our potential and an affirmation of our worthiness to receive what we seek. Integrating affirmations into a daily routine can significantly impact one's mindset, paving the way for increased abundance in all areas of life. When paired with gratitude, affirmations become even more potent, as expressing gratitude shifts our focus towards abundance rather than scarcity.

Lastly, the practice of gratitude enhances our manifestation efforts by fostering a positive mindset. When we cultivate gratitude for what we already have, we create an energetic alignment that attracts more positive experiences into our lives. Gratitude acts as a powerful magnet for abundance, amplifying our ability to manifest our desires. By incorporating gratitude practices, such as daily journaling or mindfulness, individuals can elevate their emotional vibrations, making them more receptive to the universal laws of attraction. This holistic approach to manifestation not only transforms our external circumstances but also leads to profound personal growth and fulfillment.

How Manifestation Works

Manifestation is a powerful process that involves aligning your thoughts, feelings, and actions with your desired outcomes in life. At its core, manifestation operates on the principle of the Law of Attraction, which posits that like attracts like. This means that the energy you emit through your thoughts and emotions directly influences the circumstances you attract into your life. By harnessing this universal principle, individuals can transform their desires into tangible realities. Understanding how manifestation works is crucial for anyone looking to utilize these techniques effectively in their pursuit of health, wealth, and overall success.

Visualization techniques play a pivotal role in the manifestation process. By vividly imagining your goals as if they have already been achieved, you create a mental image that serves as a blueprint for your reality. This practice not only enhances motivation but also helps in overcoming limiting beliefs that may hinder your progress. When you visualize your success, you train your mind to recognize opportunities that align with your desires, thereby increasing the likelihood of taking inspired actions that lead to your goals. Incorporating visualization into your daily routine can significantly amplify your manifestation efforts.

Daily affirmations are another essential tool in the manifestation toolkit. These positive statements help reprogram the subconscious mind, replacing negative beliefs with empowering ones. By consistently affirming your worthiness of abundance and success, you cultivate a mindset that is conducive to attracting positive experiences. Affirmations work best when they are specific, present-tense, and emotionally resonant. By integrating affirmations into your daily practice, you reinforce a belief system that supports your manifestation journey and opens doors to new possibilities.

Gratitude is a vital component of effective manifestation. By cultivating an attitude of gratitude, you raise your vibrational frequency, making you more receptive to the abundance that the universe has to offer. Expressing gratitude for what you currently have, as well as for the desires you wish to manifest, creates a powerful energetic shift. This shift aligns your emotions with the frequency of abundance, enhancing your attraction power. Integrating gratitude practices into your daily routine, such as maintaining a gratitude journal or sharing your appreciation with others, can significantly enhance your manifestation results.

Meditation practices further support the alignment with universal laws necessary for successful manifestation. Through meditation, you can quiet the mind, deepen your awareness, and connect with your inner self, allowing you to access higher states of consciousness. This enhanced awareness helps you identify and release emotional blockages that may impede your progress. Additionally, meditation fosters emotional alignment, which is crucial for manifestation. By cultivating a sense of inner peace and clarity, you can better focus your intentions and align your energy with the vibrational frequency of your desires, paving the way for their realization.

The Role of the Law of Attraction

The Law of Attraction serves as a foundational principle within the framework of manifesting health, wealth, and success. At its core, this universal law posits that like attracts like; that our thoughts, beliefs, and emotions shape our reality. By harnessing the power of positive thinking and intentional focus, individuals can align themselves with their desires and transform their lives. In "12 Steps to Success," this chapter explores how the Law of Attraction can be effectively utilized to achieve personal and professional goals, offering practical guidance and insights.

Visualization techniques play a crucial role in the application of the Law of Attraction. By vividly imagining desired outcomes, individuals can create a mental blueprint that aligns their subconscious mind with their goals. Techniques such as guided imagery and detailed visualization exercises can enhance this process, enabling practitioners to see, feel, and experience their aspirations as if they are already a reality. Engaging in this practice regularly can reprogram the mind and reinforce the belief that achieving these desires is not only possible but inevitable.

Overcoming limiting beliefs is another pivotal aspect of successfully harnessing the Law of Attraction. Many people carry subconscious beliefs that hinder their progress, often stemming from past experiences or societal conditioning. Identifying and challenging these limiting beliefs is essential for opening up to the abundance that life offers. This process involves self-reflection, journaling, and potentially working with a coach or mentor who can provide guidance in reframing these beliefs into empowering affirmations. By transforming negative thought patterns, individuals can cultivate a mindset that supports their aspirations.

Daily affirmations serve as a powerful tool in attracting abundance and success. By consistently affirming positive statements about oneself and one's goals, individuals can reinforce their intentions and build confidence. The repetition of these affirmations helps to shift the subconscious mind, fostering a sense of worthiness and attracting opportunities aligned with one's aspirations. Incorporating affirmations into daily routines can significantly enhance motivation and focus, acting as a constant reminder of one's goals and the belief that they are attainable.

Lastly, gratitude plays an indispensable role in enhancing the Law of Attraction. Cultivating a mindset of gratitude not only shifts focus from what is lacking to what is present but also raises one's vibrational frequency. Practicing gratitude daily—through journaling, meditation, or simply acknowledging the positives in life—can create a powerful resonance with abundance. When individuals express genuine appreciation for their current blessings, they open the door to receiving even more. By integrating gratitude practices into the daily routine, one can significantly amplify the effectiveness of the Law of Attraction, ultimately leading to a more fulfilled and successful life.

Chapter 2: Visualization Techniques for Manifestation

The Power of Visualization

Visualization is a powerful technique that serves as a cornerstone for manifesting desires and transforming one's life. It involves creating vivid mental images of the outcomes you wish to achieve, thereby aligning your thoughts and emotions with your goals. This practice taps into the Law of Attraction, which posits that like attracts like. By visualizing your aspirations, whether they pertain to health, wealth, or personal success, you are not only clarifying your intentions but also emotionally investing in their realization. This emotional engagement is essential because it cultivates the necessary energy to attract your desires into reality.

One of the most significant benefits of visualization is its ability to help individuals overcome limiting beliefs that often hinder progress. Many people carry subconscious doubts that dictate their self-worth and potential. Visualization serves as a direct counter to these beliefs, allowing individuals to see themselves in their desired state, be it fit, financially secure, or successful. By repeatedly envisioning this ideal self, you reprogram your subconscious mind, making it easier to break free from self-imposed limitations. This shift in mindset creates a fertile ground for the Law of Attraction to operate effectively, aligning your external reality with your internal beliefs.

In addition to visualizing outcomes, incorporating daily affirmations enhances your manifestation efforts. Affirmations are positive statements that reinforce your goals and desires, helping to solidify your belief in their attainability. When combined with visualization, affirmations amplify the emotional intensity of your practice. For instance, if you visualize a successful career while affirming, "I am deserving of success and abundance," you create a powerful synergy that boosts your manifesting power. The repetition of these affirmations, especially when spoken aloud, establishes a new narrative in your mind, one that is aligned with abundance and opportunity.

Gratitude plays a crucial role in enhancing the effects of visualization. When you express thankfulness for what you already have, you raise your vibrational frequency, making it easier to attract what you desire. Gratitude shifts your focus from lack to abundance, creating a mindset that is more receptive to receiving. By integrating gratitude into your visualization practice—perhaps by visualizing your goals while feeling a deep sense of appreciation for your current blessings—you can supercharge your manifestation efforts. This practice not only cultivates a positive attitude but also reinforces your belief in the abundance of the universe.

Finally, meditation practices can further align you with the universal laws that govern attraction and manifestation. Meditation allows for a quieting of the mind, enabling deeper connections with your intentions and aspirations. As you meditate, you can visualize your goals and allow yourself to feel the emotions associated with achieving them. This practice creates a powerful resonance that aligns your energy with the frequency of your desires. By incorporating visualization techniques, affirmations, gratitude, and meditation into a cohesive daily routine, you establish a holistic approach to manifesting success, health, and wealth. Each component reinforces the others, creating a dynamic and transformative experience that can lead to profound changes in your life.

Techniques for Effective Visualization

Visualization is a powerful technique that can significantly enhance your ability to manifest your desires and achieve success. By creating a clear mental image of your goals, you activate the Law of Attraction, aligning your energy with the outcomes you seek. The first step in effective visualization is to create a vivid and detailed mental picture of what you want to achieve. This involves engaging all your senses to make the visualization as real as possible. Picture not only the end result but also the journey and the feelings associated with achieving your goals. The more specific and immersive your visualization, the more effectively it will influence your subconscious mind.

Overcoming limiting beliefs is essential for successful visualization. Many individuals struggle to manifest their desires due to negative self-talk and deep-seated beliefs that hinder their progress. To counteract these beliefs, it's important to identify and challenge them. One effective technique is to visualize your goals while simultaneously affirming positive beliefs about your worthiness and ability to achieve them. This dual approach reinforces your visualization and helps to shift your mindset, enabling you to break free from the constraints that may have held you back in the past.

Daily affirmations play a crucial role in enhancing the effectiveness of visualization. By consistently repeating affirmations that resonate with your goals, you create a positive feedback loop that reinforces your visualizations. For instance, if your goal is to attract abundance, affirmations such as "I am worthy of abundance" or "Wealth flows easily to me" can help to reprogram your subconscious mind. Integrating these affirmations into your daily routine, perhaps during your morning rituals or before bedtime, can amplify the impact of your visualizations and keep you aligned with your intentions throughout the day.

Gratitude is another powerful tool that can enhance your visualization practice. By cultivating a sense of gratitude for what you have and for what you are in the process of manifesting, you elevate your emotional state and align your vibrations with positive outcomes. Start by maintaining a gratitude journal where you write down things you are thankful for each day, including the manifestations you are working towards. This practice not only heightens your emotional alignment but also reinforces your belief in the possibility of achieving your dreams, making your visualizations more potent.

Finally, incorporating meditation into your visualization practice can deepen your connection with universal laws. Meditation allows you to quiet your mind, focus your energy, and access a state of higher consciousness where inspiration and clarity can flow. During meditation, visualize your goals and feel the emotions associated with their achievement. This practice not only enhances your visualization but also helps you cultivate emotional alignment, a vital component of successful manifestation. By establishing a regular meditation routine, you can strengthen your ability to visualize effectively and align with the abundance and success you desire.

Real-Life Examples of Visualization Success

Real-life examples of successful visualization offer compelling evidence of the Law of Attraction and its profound impact on individuals' lives. These stories highlight the power of focused intention, creative visualization, and the transformative effects of aligning one's mindset with desired outcomes. By examining various cases, we can glean insights into how visualization techniques can be harnessed to manifest health, wealth, and success.

One notable example comes from a woman named Sarah, who struggled with chronic health issues for years. After discovering visualization techniques, she began to create vivid mental imagery of her body healing and thriving. Each day, she would spend time visualizing herself engaging in activities she loved, such as hiking and dancing. Over time, her health began to improve significantly. Sarah attributes her recovery not only to medical treatment but also to the power of visualization, which helped her overcome limiting beliefs about her body and its capabilities. Her story exemplifies how a clear vision can lead to remarkable transformations in physical health.

Another inspiring case is that of James, an aspiring entrepreneur who felt stuck in a corporate job. Frustrated with his lack of progress, he decided to create a vision board filled with images and quotes that represented his entrepreneurial dreams. By consistently engaging with this visual representation of his goals, James found himself more motivated to take actionable steps toward creating his own business. He started networking, learning new skills, and eventually launched a successful online venture. James's experience illustrates the effectiveness of vision boards as a tool for maintaining focus and clarity on one's aspirations, ultimately leading to tangible success.

The impact of daily affirmations is vividly demonstrated in the journey of Maria, who sought to attract abundance into her life. Initially plagued by self-doubt and negative thinking, she began incorporating affirmations into her morning routine. By consistently repeating statements like "I am worthy of success" and "Abundance flows to me effortlessly," she gradually shifted her mindset. Over the months, Maria noticed not only a change in her thoughts but also in her external circumstances—unexpected opportunities and financial growth began to manifest. Her story underscores the importance of emotional alignment and positive self-talk in attracting what one desires.

Lastly, the role of gratitude in enhancing attraction can be seen in the life of David, who practiced gratitude daily as part of his meditation routine. Initially focused on his struggles, he shifted his attention to the things he was grateful for, no matter how small. This practice heightened his awareness of abundance in his life and created a positive mindset. As David expressed gratitude for his current circumstances, he began to attract even more opportunities for growth and happiness. His experience highlights how gratitude not only amplifies positive feelings but also aligns individuals with the universal laws of attraction.

     DIGBY R. KERR

These real-life examples demonstrate that visualization, affirmations, gratitude, and goal-setting are not mere abstract concepts but powerful tools that can lead to extraordinary transformations. By integrating these practices into daily life, individuals can unlock their potential and manifest their desires, making tangible progress toward achieving health, wealth, and overall success. The stories of Sarah, James, Maria, and David serve as reminders that with intention, focus, and the right mindset, anyone can embark on a journey of manifestation and transformation.

Chapter 3: Overcoming Limiting Beliefs in the Law of Attraction

Identifying Limiting Beliefs

Identifying limiting beliefs is a crucial step in the journey toward manifestation and transformation. These beliefs, often deeply ingrained in our psyche, can hinder our ability to attract what we desire, whether it's health, wealth, or success. Limiting beliefs are negative thoughts or convictions that we hold about ourselves and the world around us, such as "I am not deserving of success" or "I will never be wealthy." Recognizing these beliefs is essential, as they act as barriers that prevent the Law of Attraction from working effectively in our lives. By uncovering these beliefs, we can dismantle them, paving the way for more empowering thoughts and affirmations to take root.

To identify your limiting beliefs, start by conducting a thorough self-examination. Reflect on your thoughts and feelings regarding various aspects of your life, particularly those connected to your goals. Journaling can be an effective tool for this process. Write down your aspirations and the thoughts that arise when you think about achieving them. Pay attention to any negative narratives that surface. This exercise can reveal patterns of self-doubt and fear, which are often manifestations of limiting beliefs. Once you have a clearer understanding of these beliefs, you can begin to challenge and reframe them.

It's also helpful to explore the origins of your limiting beliefs. Many of these beliefs are formed during childhood or through societal conditioning, and understanding their roots can provide insight into why they persist. Consider the messages you received from family, peers, and media about success, abundance, and self-worth. By recognizing that these beliefs are not inherently true but rather learned responses, you can start to detach from them. This process of deconstruction is vital for creating a new narrative that aligns with your aspirations and the universal laws of attraction.

Daily affirmations play a significant role in overcoming limiting beliefs. Once you have identified and acknowledged these beliefs, you can replace them with positive affirmations that reflect your desired reality. For example, if you have a belief that you are unworthy of love or success, an affirmation like "I am deserving of all the good that life has to offer" can help rewire your subconscious mind. Consistently practicing these affirmations can cultivate a mindset of abundance and positivity, reinforcing your ability to attract what you desire. It's essential to say these affirmations with conviction, allowing yourself to truly feel the emotions they evoke.

In summary, identifying limiting beliefs is a transformative process that requires introspection and honesty. By recognizing these beliefs, understanding their origins, and actively replacing them with empowering affirmations, you set the stage for a more abundant and fulfilling life. This journey not only enhances your ability to manifest your desires but also aligns you with the universal laws that govern attraction and success. As you embark on this path, remember that gratitude and emotional alignment are also essential components of effective manifestation, further enriching your experience as you work towards health, wealth, and overall success.

Techniques to Overcome Limiting Beliefs

Limiting beliefs often act as invisible barriers, hindering individuals from realizing their full potential. These deeply ingrained convictions can stem from past experiences, societal conditioning, or negative self-talk, and they can manifest in various areas of life, including health, wealth, and personal success. To transform these beliefs, it is essential to first recognize and acknowledge them. This self-awareness is the first step in a journey toward empowerment and growth. By identifying specific beliefs that hold one back, individuals can begin to challenge and dismantle them, paving the way for new, positive thought patterns.

One effective technique for overcoming limiting beliefs is visualization. This practice involves creating a mental image of the desired outcome and vividly imagining oneself achieving it. Visualization not only enhances motivation but also helps rewire the brain to accept new beliefs. For instance, if someone believes they are unworthy of success, visualizing themselves in a position of success can gradually shift this perception. By consistently engaging in this practice, individuals can create a new narrative that aligns with their goals, ultimately leading to tangible changes in their reality.

Daily affirmations are another powerful tool for overcoming limiting beliefs. These positive statements are designed to replace negative thoughts and reinforce self-worth. When repeated consistently—preferably in front of a mirror—affirmations can instill a sense of empowerment and resilience. For example, someone might affirm, "I am worthy of abundance," or "I attract positive opportunities effortlessly." By embedding these affirmations into daily routines, individuals can cultivate a mindset that is more conducive to attracting their desires, effectively rewriting the script of their lives.

Gratitude plays a crucial role in enhancing attraction and shifting limiting beliefs. By cultivating an attitude of gratitude, individuals can shift their focus from what they lack to what they have, fostering a sense of abundance. A simple daily practice of listing things one is grateful for can transform one's outlook on life and diminish feelings of scarcity. This shift not only elevates emotional alignment but also enhances one's vibrational frequency, making it easier to attract positive experiences and opportunities.

Meditation practices can further support individuals in aligning with universal laws and overcoming limiting beliefs. Through mindfulness and meditation, one can access deeper levels of self-awareness and emotional clarity. This practice allows individuals to observe their thoughts without judgment and create space for new, empowering beliefs to emerge. Combining meditation with visualization can amplify its effects, creating a powerful synergy that aligns one's inner world with their external aspirations. As individuals embrace these techniques, they will find themselves on a transformative path toward success, health, and wealth, ultimately manifesting their dreams into reality.

Transformative Stories of Belief Change

Belief change is a powerful catalyst for transformation, particularly in the context of manifestation and the Law of Attraction. When individuals shift their core beliefs, they often unlock new pathways to success, wealth, and health. This subchapter explores real-life stories of those who embarked on their journeys of belief transformation, illustrating how their experiences align with the principles of the 12 Steps to Success. By examining these narratives, readers can gain insights into the practical applications of belief change and its profound impact on attracting abundance.

One compelling story is that of Sarah, a former corporate employee who struggled with self-doubt and limiting beliefs. For years, she believed that her dreams of becoming a successful entrepreneur were unattainable. After discovering visualization techniques, Sarah began to create a vivid mental picture of her ideal life. She dedicated time each day to visualize her success, reinforcing her belief in its possibility. Over time, this practice transformed her mindset, allowing her to take actionable steps toward her goals. Sarah's story exemplifies how visualization can serve as a powerful tool for overcoming limiting beliefs and manifesting one's desires.

Another notable example is Mark, who faced financial challenges that stemmed from a scarcity mindset. He realized that his negative beliefs about money were hindering his ability to attract wealth. To combat this, Mark integrated daily affirmations into his routine. He crafted affirmations that focused on abundance and prosperity, repeating them each morning with conviction. This practice gradually rewired his thought patterns, leading to increased confidence and unexpected financial opportunities. Mark's experience highlights the impact of affirmations in reshaping beliefs and enhancing the attraction of financial success.

The role of gratitude also emerges as a significant theme in stories of belief change. Emily, a single mother, found herself overwhelmed by her circumstances and often felt stuck in a cycle of negativity. She began a gratitude journal, where she documented three things she was grateful for each day. This simple practice shifted her focus from lack to abundance, allowing her to appreciate her current situation while remaining open to new possibilities. As her outlook changed, so did her circumstances; she attracted better job opportunities and a supportive community. Emily's journey demonstrates that cultivating gratitude can enhance emotional alignment and facilitate the manifestation process.

Finally, the integration of meditation practices into daily routines has proven transformative for many individuals. James, a busy executive, struggled with stress and anxiety, which clouded his ability to align with universal laws. After committing to a regular meditation practice, he discovered a newfound clarity and peace. This shift not only improved his emotional well-being but also opened his mind to opportunities he previously overlooked. Through meditation, James was able to connect with his inner self, aligning his thoughts and actions with his goals. His story emphasizes the importance of mindfulness in the belief change process and its role in enhancing one's ability to attract success and abundance.

These transformative stories of belief change illustrate the profound impact that mindset shifts can have on personal success. By embracing visualization techniques, daily affirmations, gratitude practices, and meditation, individuals can overcome limiting beliefs and align themselves with the universal laws of attraction. Each story serves as a testament to the power of belief change, providing readers with encouragement and practical insights to start their journey toward manifestation and transformation today.

Chapter 4: Daily Affirmations and Their Impact on Attracting Abundance

The Science Behind Affirmations

The practice of affirmations has gained significant recognition in recent years, particularly within the framework of the Law of Attraction. At its core, affirmations are positive statements that individuals repeat to themselves to challenge and overcome self-sabotaging thoughts. The science behind affirmations lies in understanding how our brains process language and the profound impact that repetitive positive messaging can have on our mindset and behavior. By consistently using affirmations, we can effectively rewire our subconscious, paving the way for a more abundant and successful life.

Research in psychology highlights the phenomenon known as "cognitive restructuring," which involves changing negative thought patterns into positive ones. When we engage in affirmations, we are essentially practicing cognitive restructuring. By replacing limiting beliefs—those deep-seated thoughts that tell us we are not good enough or that success is out of reach—with empowering affirmations, we create a mental environment conducive to growth and achievement. This shift not only enhances our self-esteem but also influences our actions, leading us to pursue opportunities that align with our goals.

Moreover, neuroscience provides insights into how affirmations can affect our brain's neural pathways. Studies show that positive affirmations can activate the brain's reward centers, which are associated with feelings of joy and satisfaction. This activation encourages us to seek out experiences that reinforce our affirmations, creating a positive feedback loop. For example, if someone affirms, "I am worthy of success," the brain begins to associate that belief with feelings of happiness and motivation, making it more likely for the individual to take actionable steps toward achieving their goals.

The impact of affirmations extends beyond personal growth; they also play a significant role in enhancing emotional alignment with the Law of Attraction. When individuals consistently affirm their desires, they cultivate a mindset that is open to receiving abundance. This emotional alignment is crucial, as it influences the vibrational energy we emit into the universe. As we repeat our affirmations, we not only reinforce our beliefs but also align our emotions with those beliefs, thereby increasing our capacity to attract what we genuinely desire.

Incorporating affirmations into daily practices, such as meditation and visualization, can further amplify their effects. By combining these techniques, individuals can create a holistic approach to manifestation that harnesses both the power of positive thinking and the clarity of focused intention. As you embark on your journey toward success, consider integrating daily affirmations into your routine, allowing the science behind them to support your aspirations and transform your life. Through this commitment, you can unlock the power of your thoughts, overcome limiting beliefs, and align yourself with the abundant opportunities that await.

Crafting Effective Daily Affirmations

Crafting effective daily affirmations is a powerful tool in the journey toward manifestation and transformation. Affirmations are positive statements that help reprogram the subconscious mind, allowing individuals to overcome limiting beliefs and align with their desires. To create affirmations that resonate deeply, it's essential to use language that feels authentic and empowering. Instead of vague or generalized statements, effective affirmations should be specific, present tense, and emotionally charged. For instance, instead of saying, "I will be successful," a more impactful affirmation would be, "I am confidently achieving my goals and attracting success every day."

When crafting affirmations, it is also crucial to consider the emotional component. Affirmations should evoke feelings that align with the desired outcome. This emotional alignment enhances the effectiveness of the affirmation by creating a sense of belief and resonance. For example, if the goal is financial abundance, an affirmation like, "I am grateful for the unlimited abundance flowing into my life" not only asserts a positive belief but also engages gratitude, which is a powerful catalyst in the law of attraction. By feeling the emotions associated with the affirmation, individuals can significantly increase their vibrational frequency, making them more receptive to the opportunities and experiences that align with their intentions.

Incorporating daily affirmations into one's routine can also amplify their effectiveness. Establishing a consistent practice helps reinforce these positive statements and integrates them into daily life. This could involve reciting affirmations each morning as part of a morning ritual, writing them in a journal, or creating visual reminders around the home. The act of repetition makes the affirmations more ingrained in the subconscious, facilitating a gradual shift in mindset. Engaging in visualization techniques while affirming can further enhance this practice—imagining oneself living out the affirmations can create a stronger sense of reality around them.

Moreover, it is essential to tailor affirmations to address specific limiting beliefs that may hinder progress toward goals. By identifying these beliefs, individuals can create counter-affirmations that directly challenge and transform them. For instance, if a person struggles with self-doubt about their abilities, an affirmation like, "I trust in my skills and abilities to achieve my dreams" can counteract negative self-talk. This process not only helps in overcoming internal obstacles but also empowers individuals to take proactive steps toward their aspirations, fostering a mindset of resilience and strength.

Lastly, the impact of gratitude cannot be overstated in the context of daily affirmations. By incorporating gratitude into affirmations, individuals can enhance their attraction to positive experiences. Statements such as, "I am thankful for the abundance and opportunities that surround me" not only express appreciation but also align with the universal laws of attraction. This synergy between affirmations and gratitude creates a powerful momentum that propels individuals toward their goals, reinforcing the belief that they are deserving of success and abundance. By embracing this holistic approach, individuals can craft affirmations that not only resonate deeply but also serve as a foundation for their journey toward manifestation and transformation.

Success Stories: Affirmations in Action

The power of affirmations is a crucial element in the journey toward manifestation and transformation. Numerous individuals have harnessed the strength of positive self-talk to overcome challenges and align themselves with their goals. These success stories highlight how daily affirmations can serve as a catalyst for change, enabling people to break free from limiting beliefs and attract the abundance they desire. By sharing these real-life applications, readers can draw inspiration and practical insights to incorporate affirmations into their own lives effectively.

One remarkable example is that of Jenna, a graphic designer who struggled with self-doubt and financial insecurity. Jenna began her day by reciting affirmations focused on her capabilities and the abundance available to her. Phrases such as "I am worthy of financial success" and "My creativity flows effortlessly" became part of her morning routine. Within a few months, Jenna not only gained confidence in her abilities but also attracted new clients who recognized her talent. This transformation illustrates how affirmations can shift one's mindset and open doors to opportunities previously thought unattainable.

In another inspiring story, Marcus, an entrepreneur, faced numerous setbacks while launching his startup. Frustrated and on the verge of giving up, he decided to integrate affirmations into his daily routine. By repeating affirmations like "I attract success effortlessly" and "Every setback is a setup for a comeback," Marcus began to alter his outlook. As he embraced this new mindset, he noticed increased clarity in decision-making and a stronger focus on his goals. Eventually, his startup gained traction, leading to partnerships and financial success that he once only dreamed of. Marcus's experience underscores the profound impact that affirmations can have on fostering resilience and enhancing one's ability to manifest desires.

The role of gratitude in conjunction with affirmations also plays a pivotal part in these success stories. Sarah, a wellness coach, incorporated daily affirmations of gratitude alongside her usual practice. By expressing thankfulness for her current achievements and the abundance she anticipated, she cultivated a positive emotional state that reinforced her affirmations. This synergy between gratitude and positive affirmations led Sarah to attract new clients and opportunities for growth. Her story exemplifies how integrating gratitude can amplify the effectiveness of affirmations, creating a powerful momentum for manifestation.

In conclusion, the stories of Jenna, Marcus, and Sarah illustrate that affirmations are more than mere words; they are powerful tools for transformation. By consistently practicing daily affirmations and aligning them with gratitude, individuals can dismantle limiting beliefs and pave the way for success. As readers embark on their journey through the 12 Steps to Success, these real-life examples serve as a testament to the effectiveness of affirmations in action. With commitment and the right mindset, anyone can harness the power of affirmations to manifest their dreams and achieve their desired reality.

Chapter 5: The Role of Gratitude in Enhancing Attraction

Understanding Gratitude's Power

Understanding the power of gratitude is essential for anyone on the journey of manifestation and transformation. Gratitude serves as a catalyst for attracting positive experiences and abundance into our lives. When we cultivate an attitude of gratitude, we align ourselves with the energy of abundance, which is fundamental to the Law of Attraction. This energy shifts our focus from what we lack to what we already possess, creating a fertile ground for further manifestations. By recognizing and appreciating the blessings in our lives, we not only elevate our emotional state but also signal to the universe that we are ready to receive more.

Incorporating gratitude into daily routines can significantly enhance the effectiveness of visualization techniques used in manifestation. When we visualize our desires, combining this practice with gratitude amplifies its power. For instance, when visualizing a successful outcome, expressing gratitude for that success as if it has already occurred creates a strong emotional resonance. This emotional alignment is crucial, as the Law of Attraction operates on the principle that like attracts like. By feeling gratitude in advance, we align our vibration with that of our desires, making it easier for them to manifest.

Overcoming limiting beliefs is another critical aspect of harnessing gratitude's power. Many individuals struggle with self-doubt and negative thoughts that hinder their ability to attract what they want. Gratitude acts as a powerful antidote to these limiting beliefs. When we focus on what we appreciate in our lives, we begin to challenge the narratives that hold us back. Affirmations become more potent when grounded in gratitude; for example, affirming, "I am grateful for the abundance flowing into my life" helps to rewire subconscious beliefs. This practice not only fosters a positive mindset but also reinforces the idea that abundance is our natural state.

Daily affirmations and gratitude can work hand in hand to create a robust framework for attracting wealth and success. By starting each day with a gratitude practice, individuals can set a positive tone for the day. This could be as simple as listing three things they are grateful for or reflecting on positive experiences. Following this with affirmations that resonate with their goals integrates gratitude into their manifestation practices. This combination cultivates a mindset of abundance, making it easier to overcome challenges and maintain focus on long-term goals.

Finally, the role of gratitude in meditation practices cannot be overstated. Meditation provides a space to cultivate mindfulness and connect with one's inner self, while gratitude enhances this experience. By incorporating gratitude into meditation, individuals can deepen their emotional alignment with their desires. Techniques such as focusing on feelings of gratitude during meditation can help clear mental clutter and enhance clarity on what one truly wants. This practice not only aligns individuals with the universal laws of attraction but also fosters a sense of peace and fulfillment, paving the way for transformative experiences. Embracing gratitude as a core component of the manifestation process can lead to profound changes in health, wealth, and overall success.

Daily Gratitude Practices

Daily gratitude practices serve as a powerful tool in the journey of manifestation and transformation. By acknowledging and appreciating what we already have, we create a positive emotional state that aligns us with the universal laws of attraction. Gratitude shifts our focus from lack to abundance, enabling us to cultivate a mindset that is receptive to the good that life has to offer. This foundational step is not only essential for attracting wealth, health, and success but also plays a crucial role in overcoming limiting beliefs that often hinder our progress.

Incorporating daily gratitude into your routine can be simple yet profoundly impactful. Start each day by writing down three things you are grateful for, no matter how small they may seem. This practice helps to set a positive tone for the day ahead and encourages a mindset of abundance. Additionally, consider keeping a gratitude journal, where you can reflect on your experiences and the blessings you encounter. Over time, this consistent practice will not only enhance your emotional alignment with your desires but can also serve as a motivational tool, reminding you of the progress you've made in your life.

To deepen the effects of gratitude on your manifestation journey, combine it with daily affirmations. Affirmations are positive statements that reinforce your beliefs and intentions. When you express gratitude for your current circumstances while simultaneously affirming your aspirations, you create a powerful resonance that attracts your desired outcomes. For instance, saying, "I am grateful for the abundance I have and the wealth that is flowing to me effortlessly" combines the vibrational energies of gratitude and intention, amplifying your manifesting abilities.

Meditation practices also enhance your gratitude practice by allowing you to connect with your inner self and align with universal laws. Taking a few moments each day to meditate on your blessings can deepen your appreciation and enhance your emotional state. Visualization techniques can further elevate this practice; as you meditate, visualize the things you are grateful for and the abundance you wish to attract. This combination of gratitude and visualization can create a potent energy that resonates with the universe, making it more likely for your desires to manifest.

Lastly, consider integrating gratitude into other spiritual practices such as creating vision boards or exploring the science behind the law of attraction. A vision board filled with images and words that represent your goals can be enriched by including elements of gratitude. By consciously acknowledging what you are thankful for while visualizing your future, you bridge the gap between where you are and where you want to be. This holistic approach, rooted in gratitude, not only strengthens your manifestation journey but also cultivates a deeper sense of fulfillment and joy in your everyday life.

Real-Life Transformations through Gratitude

Real-life transformations through gratitude can serve as powerful testimonies to the effectiveness of the Law of Attraction. Gratitude acts as a catalyst for positive change, fostering an environment where abundance can flourish. By recognizing and appreciating what we already have, we align ourselves with the energy of abundance, making it easier to attract even more positive experiences. The act of giving thanks not only elevates our mood but also shifts our focus from what is lacking to what is present, creating a fertile ground for manifestation.

One profound example of transformation through gratitude can be found in the story of Jane, a once-struggling entrepreneur who faced daily challenges in her business. Overwhelmed by self-doubt and limiting beliefs, Jane decided to implement a daily gratitude practice. Each morning, she would write down three things she was grateful for, ranging from small victories to the support of her loved ones. This simple act gradually shifted her mindset, allowing her to recognize the opportunities around her. As her perspective changed, so did her business; she began attracting clients and partnerships that had previously eluded her, demonstrating how gratitude can transform one's reality.

Similarly, gratitude has played a pivotal role in the journey of Tom, who struggled with financial instability. After years of negative thinking and feeling stuck, Tom discovered the power of daily affirmations combined with gratitude. He created a list of affirmations focusing on abundance and success, but he also included a gratitude component, thanking the universe for the wealth he was about to receive. This dual practice not only reinforced his belief in the Law of Attraction but also helped him overcome limiting beliefs that had kept him from pursuing new opportunities. Tom's financial situation transformed dramatically as he embraced this new mindset, leading to a significant increase in his income and overall well-being.

Incorporating gratitude into meditation practices can further enhance its transformative effects. When individuals meditate with a focus on gratitude, they cultivate a deeper emotional alignment with their desires. This practice encourages the release of negative energies and invites a sense of peace and contentment, which are essential for successful manifestation. By visualizing their goals while expressing gratitude, practitioners can create a vivid mental image of their desired outcomes, solidifying their intentions in the universe. Many have reported profound changes in their lives after adopting this combined approach, experiencing a clearer path toward their aspirations.

Creating vision boards that incorporate elements of gratitude can also significantly enhance the manifestation process. By visually representing their goals alongside images and words that evoke feelings of thankfulness, individuals can maintain a constant reminder of what they aspire to achieve. This visual representation serves as a daily affirmation of gratitude, reinforcing positive beliefs and attracting abundance. Success stories abound of those who have utilized this technique, finding that their vision boards not only inspire action but also foster a sense of joy and appreciation for the journey toward their goals. In essence, gratitude acts as both the fuel and the compass, guiding individuals on their path to success.

Chapter 6: Meditation Practices for Aligning with Universal Laws

Types of Meditation for Manifestation

Meditation serves as a powerful tool for manifestation, enabling individuals to align their thoughts and emotions with their desires. Various types of meditation can facilitate this process, each catering to different aspects of manifestation. Understanding these different meditation techniques is crucial for anyone looking to harness the Law of Attraction effectively. By exploring these methods, practitioners can find the most suitable approach to foster their intentions and manifest their dreams.

One of the most common forms of meditation for manifestation is visualization meditation. This technique involves creating vivid mental images of one's goals and desires. By engaging all the senses and imagining the experience of achieving these goals, practitioners can strengthen their emotional connection to their desired outcomes. Visualization not only enhances clarity of purpose but also activates the subconscious mind to recognize opportunities that align with these intentions. Regular practice of visualization meditation can dramatically increase the likelihood of attracting desired outcomes by embedding them into the practitioner's mindset.

Another effective meditation approach is affirmations meditation. This method involves repeating positive statements that reinforce one's beliefs about success, abundance, and self-worth. By integrating affirmations into a meditative practice, individuals can overcome limiting beliefs that often hinder manifestation efforts. This form of meditation helps to reprogram the subconscious mind, replacing negative thought patterns with empowering beliefs. As a result, practitioners can cultivate a mindset that is not only open to receiving but also confident in their ability to manifest their desires.

Gratitude meditation is another powerful technique that enhances the manifestation process. By focusing on feelings of gratitude, individuals can shift their emotional state and align themselves with the frequency of abundance. This practice encourages a deeper appreciation for what one already has while simultaneously opening the door to future blessings. Regularly engaging in gratitude meditation can create a positive feedback loop, where the practice itself attracts more reasons to be grateful, thereby amplifying the manifestation process.

Lastly, mindfulness meditation can play a significant role in manifestation by fostering emotional alignment. This practice encourages individuals to become aware of their thoughts and feelings without judgment, allowing them to identify and release any resistance to their desires. By cultivating a state of presence and acceptance, practitioners can align their emotional energy with their intentions. This alignment is crucial in the Law of Attraction, as it ensures that one's thoughts, feelings, and actions are in harmony, ultimately paving the way for successful manifestation. Integrating these meditation practices into a daily routine can significantly enhance the effectiveness of the manifestation journey, making it easier to attract health, wealth, and success.

Creating a Meditation Routine

Creating a meditation routine is an essential step in aligning with the principles of the Law of Attraction. This subchapter will guide you through the process of establishing a consistent meditation practice that enhances your ability to manifest health, wealth, and success. By dedicating time each day to quiet your mind and focus your energy, you can cultivate a deeper connection with the universal laws that govern attraction. This routine not only fosters emotional alignment but also prepares you to receive the abundance you seek.

Begin by selecting a specific time each day for your meditation practice. Consistency is key, as it helps to create a habit that becomes an integral part of your daily routine. Whether you prefer mornings, when your mind is fresh, or evenings, to reflect on your day, choose a time that feels natural. Start with just five to ten minutes a day, gradually increasing the duration as you become more comfortable. This allows you to ease into meditation without feeling overwhelmed, making it more likely that you will stick with it.

Next, create a dedicated space for your meditation. This doesn't need to be elaborate; a quiet corner with minimal distractions will suffice. Consider adding elements that inspire focus and relaxation, such as cushions, candles, or calming music. The goal is to create an environment that signals to your mind and body that it's time to enter a state of calm and introspection. Incorporating visualization techniques during your meditation can also be highly effective. Picture your goals and desires as if they are already in your life, using this mental imagery to reinforce your intentions.

Incorporating daily affirmations into your meditation can further enhance your manifestation efforts. Choose affirmations that resonate with your goals, such as "I am worthy of abundance" or "I attract success effortlessly." Repeat these affirmations silently or aloud during your meditation, allowing their positive energy to permeate your subconscious mind. This practice helps to overcome limiting beliefs that may be hindering your progress, reinforcing the notion that you are capable of achieving your dreams.

Finally, expressing gratitude during your meditation can amplify your connection to the Law of Attraction. Take a moment to reflect on the blessings you currently have in your life, no matter how small. This practice not only shifts your mindset to one of abundance but also raises your vibrational frequency, making it easier to attract what you desire. By establishing a meditation routine that combines these elements—dedicated time, a peaceful space, visualization, affirmations, and gratitude—you position yourself to harness the full power of the universe in your journey toward success.

Personal Stories of Meditation and Success

In the journey toward success and personal transformation, meditation serves as a powerful tool that many individuals have harnessed to align with their desires and aspirations. The practice of meditation not only cultivates mindfulness but also enhances one's ability to visualize goals clearly. Numerous success stories illustrate how individuals have used meditation as a foundational practice to manifest their dreams. By creating a quiet space for reflection, meditation allows people to connect with their inner selves, fostering clarity and purpose, which are essential for effective manifestation.

One compelling story involves a young entrepreneur who struggled with self-doubt and limiting beliefs. After discovering the Law of Attraction, she began incorporating daily meditation into her routine. Through guided visualizations, she confronted her fears and visualized her success vividly. This practice not only helped her to overcome her limiting beliefs but also opened her mind to new opportunities. The transformation was evident—her business began to thrive, and she credits her meditation practice as the catalyst for her newfound confidence and success.

In another instance, a corporate professional faced burnout and dissatisfaction in her career. Seeking change, she turned to daily affirmations combined with meditation. Each morning, she would meditate on her affirmations, which centered around abundance and fulfillment. This practice not only shifted her mindset but also attracted new career opportunities that aligned with her values. The impact of her daily routine extended beyond her professional life; she found herself more grateful and open to experiences, reinforcing the idea that gratitude enhances the Law of Attraction.

The role of gratitude in meditation cannot be overstated. One participant in a meditation workshop shared how he began to incorporate gratitude into his practice. By dedicating a portion of his meditation to reflect on what he was thankful for, he discovered a profound shift in his overall outlook. This shift not only attracted positive relationships but also led to unexpected financial gains. His story serves as a testament to how gratitude, when combined with meditation, can amplify the effects of the Law of Attraction, creating a cycle of abundance and success.

Lastly, the integration of meditation with other spiritual practices can create a holistic approach to personal development. One individual shared how he combined meditation with vision board creation, setting clear intentions for his future. By meditating on his vision board, he was able to visualize his goals deeply and embed them into his subconscious. This dual practice enabled him to manifest significant life changes, including a fulfilling career and enriching relationships. These personal stories highlight the multifaceted benefits of meditation, illustrating its power as a transformative practice that complements the principles of manifestation and the Law of Attraction.

Chapter 7: Creating Vision Boards: A Step-by-Step Guide

The Purpose of Vision Boards

The concept of vision boards has gained significant traction in personal development and manifestation circles, serving as a powerful tool for visualizing goals and aspirations. A vision board is essentially a visual representation of your dreams and objectives, crafted from images, words, and symbols that resonate with your desired outcomes. By creating a tangible collage of what you wish to attract into your life—be it health, wealth, success, or personal fulfillment—you engage in a process that enhances focus and clarity. This practice aligns with the principles of the Law of Attraction, which posits that like attracts like; thus, by visualizing your goals, you begin to attract experiences and opportunities that will help you achieve them.

One of the primary purposes of a vision board is to serve as a daily reminder of your intentions and aspirations. In a world filled with distractions and challenges, having a physical representation of your goals can help maintain motivation and mental clarity. This constant visual stimulus can reinforce your commitment, reminding you of the steps you need to take to manifest your desires. By integrating this tool into your daily routine, you can overcome limiting beliefs that may hinder your progress, as the images and affirmations on your board challenge your subconscious to expand its boundaries and embrace new possibilities.

Moreover, vision boards encourage the practice of daily affirmations—another vital element in the manifestation process. When you regularly affirm your goals and visualize them on your board, you create a positive feedback loop that enhances your emotional alignment with your desires. This emotional resonance is crucial for effective manifestation, as it fosters a sense of deservingness and abundance. By consistently engaging with your vision board, you can cultivate a mindset that not only attracts opportunities but also prepares you to recognize and seize them when they arise.

Gratitude plays a pivotal role in amplifying the effectiveness of vision boards. When you express gratitude for what you have while visualizing what you want, you create a powerful emotional state that aligns with abundance. This practice not only helps in overcoming scarcity mindsets but also elevates your vibration, making it easier for you to attract your desired outcomes. Incorporating gratitude into your vision board practice—perhaps by including images or phrases that express thankfulness—can deepen your connection to your goals and enhance your overall manifestation journey.

Finally, the process of creating a vision board can be therapeutic and introspective, allowing you to clarify your values and priorities. By thoughtfully selecting images and materials that resonate with your true desires, you engage in a self-discovery process that can lead to profound personal transformation. This practice not only aligns with other spiritual practices, such as meditation, but also reinforces the importance of emotional alignment in manifestation. As you create and interact with your vision board, you invite the universal laws to work in harmony with your intentions, paving the way for transformative experiences that can lead to health, wealth, and success in your life.

Materials and Techniques for Vision Boards

Materials and techniques for creating vision boards play a crucial role in harnessing the power of visualization and manifestation. A vision board serves as a tangible representation of your aspirations, dreams, and goals, acting as a daily reminder of what you wish to attract into your life. To begin your vision board journey, it's essential to gather the right materials. Common items include a sturdy poster board or corkboard, magazines or printed images, scissors, glue or pushpins, and markers. You can also consider incorporating digital tools such as apps like Pinterest or Canva for a tech-savvy approach, allowing for more flexibility and creativity in designing your vision board.

Selecting the images and words that resonate with your goals is a pivotal step in the vision board process. For effective manifestation, choose visuals that evoke strong emotions and reflect your desires accurately. This could range from images of your dream home, travel destinations, or representations of financial success. Complementing these images with powerful affirmations or quotes can enhance the board's impact. Writing down specific, positive statements related to your goals reinforces your intentions while helping to overcome limiting beliefs. The combination of visual and textual elements creates a dynamic focal point that aligns with the principles of the Law of Attraction.

Once the materials are assembled and the visuals selected, it's time to arrange them on your board. The layout should be intuitive and reflect your personal style. You may choose to categorize your goals—such as health, wealth, relationships, and personal growth—or opt for a more freeform design. The placement of each image and affirmation is significant; arrange them in a way that draws your eye and allows you to absorb the energy of your aspirations. Consider using colors that resonate with the emotions you want to evoke, as color psychology can play an influential role in your mindset and emotional alignment.

After your vision board is complete, the next technique involves incorporating the board into your daily routine. Place it in a location you frequent, such as your bedroom, office, or meditation space, ensuring that it remains a constant reminder of your intentions. Engage with your vision board daily by taking a few moments to visualize your goals as if they are already achieved. This practice aligns your energy with your desires, fostering a mindset that is open to receiving abundance. Additionally, consider integrating gratitude into this process; regularly acknowledging the progress you make and the blessings you already have can amplify your manifestation efforts.

Finally, the effectiveness of your vision board can be enhanced by combining it with other spiritual practices, such as meditation and affirmations. Meditation allows you to clear your mind and focus on the feelings associated with your goals, while daily affirmations reinforce a positive mindset. By integrating gratitude practices and these meditative techniques with your vision board, you create a holistic approach to manifestation. This multifaceted strategy not only supports emotional alignment but also strengthens your belief in the Law of Attraction, paving the way for real-life transformations and success.

Transformative Stories from Vision Board Users

Vision boards have emerged as powerful tools for manifestation, enabling individuals to visualize their dreams and bring them to fruition. Many users have reported profound transformations in their lives after creating and consistently engaging with their vision boards. These stories illustrate the practical application of visualization techniques and how they can help overcome limiting beliefs, ultimately aligning individuals with their desires and aspirations.

One notable account comes from Sarah, a graphic designer who felt stuck in her career. After attending a workshop on the Law of Attraction, she decided to create a vision board filled with images and affirmations related to her professional goals. Each day, Sarah spent time visualizing her success in her dream job. Within a few months, she received an unexpected job offer that perfectly aligned with her vision. This experience not only transformed her career but also reinforced her belief in the power of daily affirmations and visualization techniques. Sarah's story exemplifies how a vision board can serve as a tangible representation of one's goals, making it easier to manifest them.

Another inspiring story is that of James, who struggled with financial insecurity. After learning about the significance of gratitude and emotional alignment in the manifestation process, he created a vision board that included images of abundance and affirmations reflecting his financial goals. By incorporating daily gratitude practices, James shifted his mindset from scarcity to abundance. Over time, he noticed significant changes in his financial situation, including unexpected income and new opportunities. His journey highlights the essential role of gratitude in enhancing attraction and how a vision board can help maintain focus on abundance rather than lack.

Additionally, Maria, a wellness coach, shared her experience of using a vision board to align her personal and professional aspirations. She integrated meditation practices with her vision board, spending time in quiet reflection while visualizing her goals. This combination allowed her to connect deeply with her desires, fostering emotional alignment and boosting her confidence. As a result, Maria launched a successful online wellness program that resonated with her vision. Her success story underscores the importance of combining various spiritual practices, such as meditation and visualization, to amplify the effects of the Law of Attraction.

These transformative stories from vision board users illustrate the profound impact that visualization and positive thinking can have on one's life. By overcoming limiting beliefs, practicing daily affirmations, and cultivating gratitude, individuals can create a powerful foundation for manifesting their dreams. As these real-life applications of the 12 steps reveal, vision boards serve not only as a source of inspiration but also as a practical guide for aligning with universal laws and attracting the health, wealth, and success that one desires.

Chapter 8: The Science Behind the Law of Attraction

Research Supporting the Law of Attraction

The Law of Attraction has garnered considerable attention over the years, not only in self-help circles but also within scientific communities that seek to understand its principles and efficacy. Research supporting the Law of Attraction often draws on fields such as psychology and neuroscience, which provide insights into how thoughts, beliefs, and emotions can shape our realities. By examining cognitive patterns and behavioral responses, researchers have begun to unveil the mechanisms that underpin this powerful law, affirming that our mental frameworks significantly influence our experiences and outcomes in life.

One of the key components of the Law of Attraction is the practice of visualization, which has been shown to have profound effects on achieving personal goals. Studies have indicated that mental imagery can enhance performance in various domains, from sports to academics. This phenomenon occurs because visualization activates the same neural pathways that physical practice does, reinforcing the belief that one's goals are attainable. By employing visualization techniques, individuals can create a mental blueprint of their desired outcomes, effectively aligning their subconscious mind with their conscious aspirations.

Overcoming limiting beliefs is another critical area where research intersects with the Law of Attraction. Cognitive-behavioral therapy (CBT) has demonstrated that challenging negative thought patterns can lead to significant shifts in behavior and emotional well-being. This aligns with the Law of Attraction's emphasis on maintaining a positive mindset. By identifying and reframing limiting beliefs, individuals can break free from self-imposed barriers, allowing them to attract the health, wealth, and success they desire. This process not only enhances self-efficacy but also opens up new pathways for manifestation.

Daily affirmations and their impact on attracting abundance have also been substantiated through various studies. Affirmations work by countering negative self-talk and reinforcing positive beliefs. Research in psychology indicates that consistent affirmation can lead to improved self-esteem and a greater sense of agency. By integrating daily affirmations into their routines, individuals can cultivate a more abundant mindset, thereby enhancing their ability to attract positive experiences and opportunities in their lives. This practice serves as a powerful reminder of the potential for transformation inherent in each person.

Gratitude plays a pivotal role in the Law of Attraction, with research highlighting its psychological benefits. Numerous studies have shown that practicing gratitude can lead to increased well-being and greater life satisfaction. When individuals focus on what they are thankful for, they shift their attention away from scarcity and negativity, creating a positive emotional state that is conducive to attracting abundance. By incorporating gratitude into their daily lives, individuals not only enhance their emotional alignment with their goals but also signal to the universe their readiness to receive more of what they desire. This synergy between gratitude and the Law of Attraction further underscores the importance of emotional alignment in the manifestation process.

Understanding Quantum Physics and Manifestation

Understanding Quantum Physics and Manifestation delves into the intriguing relationship between the principles of quantum physics and the art of manifestation. At its core, quantum physics explores the behavior of matter and energy at the smallest scales, revealing a world that operates fundamentally differently from our everyday experiences. This subchapter will illustrate how these scientific principles can empower individuals to harness the Law of Attraction, transforming their aspirations into reality by aligning their thoughts, emotions, and actions with the universal energies around them.

One of the pivotal concepts in quantum physics is the idea that everything is interconnected. This principle aligns seamlessly with the Law of Attraction, which posits that like attracts like. Just as quantum particles can instantaneously affect one another regardless of distance, our thoughts and emotions can influence the universe and attract corresponding experiences into our lives. By understanding this connection, individuals can begin to shift their focus from limiting beliefs to abundant possibilities. This shift is crucial for overcoming barriers that may impede their manifestation journey.

Visualization techniques play a significant role in connecting the principles of quantum physics with the practice of manifestation. When individuals visualize their desired outcomes, they are essentially engaging in a form of quantum creation. This technique harnesses the brain's ability to create new neural pathways, allowing the mind to perceive success as a tangible reality. By vividly imagining their goals and feeling the emotions associated with achieving them, individuals can set into motion the quantum processes that align their energy with their desires. This practice can be enhanced through daily affirmations, which reinforce positive beliefs and further solidify the mental framework necessary for attracting abundance.

Gratitude also plays a critical role in enhancing attraction, serving as a powerful emotional state that aligns one's energy with the universe. Quantum physics suggests that energy vibrates at different frequencies, and gratitude is one of the highest vibrations. By cultivating a practice of gratitude, individuals elevate their emotional state, attracting more of what they appreciate into their lives. This emotional alignment is essential for successful manifestation, as it resonates with the universal laws governing attraction and abundance.

Finally, integrating meditation practices into this framework can deepen one's understanding of both quantum physics and manifestation. Meditation fosters a state of clarity and presence, allowing individuals to tap into the universal consciousness that quantum physics hints at. This state of awareness enables practitioners to align their thoughts and emotions with their true desires, facilitating a more profound connection to the Law of Attraction. Creating vision boards, another effective tool for manifestation, can visually anchor these intentions, providing a daily reminder of one's goals. By merging the insights of quantum physics with practical manifestation techniques, individuals can embark on a transformative journey toward health, wealth, and success.

Scientific Success Stories

In the realm of manifestation and transformation, scientific success stories provide a compelling backdrop that showcases the intersection of evidence-based research and the principles of the Law of Attraction. These narratives highlight how individuals have effectively harnessed visualization techniques and daily affirmations to reshape their realities and overcome limiting beliefs. By examining these stories, readers can glean practical insights into how scientific principles support the tenets of manifestation, encouraging a deeper understanding and application of the 12 steps outlined in this guide.

One notable example is the work conducted by psychologists who have studied the impact of visualization on performance outcomes. Research shows that athletes who engage in mental imagery can enhance their physical performance significantly. This scientific validation of visualization techniques aligns with the concept that visualizing success can create a powerful mental blueprint that guides individuals toward their goals. By incorporating these findings into daily practices, readers can utilize visualization to manifest their desires more effectively, reinforcing the idea that the mind is a vital tool in the process of attraction.

Overcoming limiting beliefs is another critical facet of the manifestation journey, and numerous studies have explored the effectiveness of cognitive restructuring in this regard. Individuals who challenge and reframe their negative thoughts have reported increased self-efficacy and improved outcomes in various aspects of life, including health and relationships. These findings resonate with the Law of Attraction's core principle: that our thoughts directly influence our reality. By sharing real-life success stories of those who have transformed their beliefs, this section aims to inspire readers to confront and dismantle their own mental barriers, thus facilitating a more profound connection with the universal laws governing attraction.

Gratitude, too, plays a pivotal role in enhancing attraction, with numerous studies indicating its positive impact on mental and emotional well-being. Practicing gratitude has been linked to increased levels of happiness and satisfaction in life, which are essential for aligning with abundance. Success stories from individuals who have adopted gratitude as a daily practice illustrate how this simple yet profound shift in perspective can lead to transformative experiences. By integrating gratitude into their daily routines, readers can elevate their emotional states, making them more receptive to attracting wealth, health, and success.

Finally, the science behind meditation practices reveals their effectiveness in aligning individuals with universal laws. Research supports the notion that mindfulness and meditation can lead to improved focus, emotional regulation, and overall well-being. Success stories abound of people who have incorporated meditation into their lives, resulting in not just a deeper connection with their inner selves but also tangible external results. This subchapter underscores the importance of integrating meditation with other spiritual practices, highlighting how a holistic approach can amplify the results of the 12 steps to success. By embracing these scientific success stories, readers can find inspiration and guidance on their unique paths to manifestation and transformation.

Chapter 9: Integrating the Law of Attraction with Other Spiritual Practices

Complementary Spiritual Practices

Complementary spiritual practices play a vital role in enhancing the effectiveness of the Law of Attraction and manifesting desired outcomes in life. While many are familiar with the core principles of visualization, affirmations, and gratitude, integrating these practices can create a more holistic approach to achieving health, wealth, and success. This subchapter aims to explore various complementary practices that can be seamlessly woven into daily routines, thus amplifying the manifestation process.

Visualization techniques are one of the most powerful tools in the manifestation arsenal. By vividly imagining desired outcomes, individuals can create a mental blueprint that guides their actions and mindset. To maximize the effectiveness of visualization, it is essential to engage all the senses. For instance, instead of merely picturing a new job, one should envision the sounds of the workplace, the feeling of a new desk, and even the scent of fresh coffee. This multi-sensory approach deepens emotional engagement, making the envisioned reality feel more attainable and real.

Overcoming limiting beliefs is another critical aspect of successful manifestation. Many individuals unknowingly sabotage their efforts by holding onto negative beliefs about themselves or their capabilities. It is essential to identify and challenge these beliefs actively. Journaling can be a helpful practice in this regard; by writing down limiting thoughts and reframing them into positive affirmations, individuals can shift their mindset. For example, transforming "I am not good enough" into "I am worthy of success" can create a profound shift in perception, allowing for greater alignment with the universal laws of attraction.

Daily affirmations serve as a practical tool for reinforcing positive beliefs and attracting abundance. By repeating affirmations consistently, individuals can rewire their subconscious minds, paving the way for new possibilities. These affirmations should be specific and resonate deeply with personal aspirations. For instance, instead of a generic statement like "I attract wealth," one could use "I am open to receiving unexpected financial opportunities." This specificity helps to create a strong emotional connection and aligns energy with the desired outcome, making it easier to attract what one truly desires.

Gratitude is a foundational practice that enhances the effectiveness of all manifestations. By cultivating an attitude of gratitude, individuals raise their vibrational frequency, making them more receptive to abundance. Keeping a gratitude journal, where one writes down daily things they are thankful for, can shift focus from lack to abundance. Additionally, incorporating gratitude into visualization and affirmation practices can create a powerful synergy. For example, while visualizing a desired outcome, expressing gratitude for it as if it has already manifested can amplify the feeling of abundance and enhance the attraction process.

Meditation practices also play a crucial role in aligning oneself with universal laws. Regular meditation helps to quiet the mind, reduce stress, and create a deeper connection to one's inner self. This connection fosters emotional alignment, which is essential for successful manifestation. Techniques such as mindfulness meditation can enhance awareness of thoughts and emotions, allowing individuals to recognize and release negativity. Moreover, guided meditations focused on abundance can help establish a clear intention and solidify the belief that one is deserving of all good things. By integrating these complementary spiritual practices, individuals can create a robust framework for manifesting health, wealth, and overall success.

Creating a Holistic Approach to Manifestation

Creating a holistic approach to manifestation involves intertwining various techniques and practices that not only align with the Law of Attraction but also enhance one's overall well-being. This comprehensive method emphasizes the interconnectedness of mind, body, and spirit, ensuring that individuals are not only focused on their goals but are also nurturing their emotional and physical health. By integrating visualization techniques, daily affirmations, gratitude practices, and meditation, one can create a balanced pathway for attracting health, wealth, and success.

Visualization techniques form a crucial component of this holistic approach. By vividly imagining one's desired outcomes, individuals can harness the power of their subconscious mind to attract those realities into their lives. This practice involves not just mental imagery but also engaging the senses to create a more profound experience. For example, when visualizing a successful career, it is beneficial to picture the office environment, hear the sounds of colleagues, and feel the excitement of achieving goals. This multi-sensory experience reinforces the belief in the possibility of manifestation, making it easier to overcome limiting beliefs that may hinder progress.

Daily affirmations serve as another vital tool in the manifestation process. These positive statements can shift one's mindset and reinforce self-belief, which is essential in overcoming self-doubt and negativity. Crafting personalized affirmations that resonate deeply with individual goals can create a strong emotional alignment with the desired outcomes. By consistently repeating these affirmations, individuals actively engage in reprogramming their subconscious mind, aligning their thoughts with their intentions. This practice not only promotes confidence but also fosters a sense of empowerment, making it easier to take inspired action toward one's goals.

Gratitude plays a pivotal role in enhancing attraction by fostering a positive emotional state. When individuals practice gratitude, they shift their focus from lack to abundance, creating an energetic alignment with the frequency of what they desire. This practice can be simple yet powerful; keeping a gratitude journal or expressing appreciation for small daily blessings can significantly elevate one's vibration. As individuals cultivate an attitude of gratitude, they naturally attract more positive experiences and opportunities into their lives, reinforcing the belief that abundance is not only possible but already present in their lives.

Finally, integrating meditation practices into a holistic approach to manifestation allows individuals to tap into a deeper state of awareness and connection with universal laws. Meditation helps quiet the mind, promoting clarity and focus on one's intentions. It also serves to align emotions with desires, ensuring that individuals are not only thinking about their goals but truly feeling them as if they have already been achieved. By incorporating these various elements—visualization, affirmations, gratitude, and meditation—into a daily routine, individuals can create a robust framework for manifestation that addresses all aspects of their being, paving the way for genuine transformation and success.

Case Studies of Integrated Practices

In the journey toward manifesting health, wealth, and success, integrating various practices can significantly enhance the effectiveness of the Law of Attraction. This subchapter presents compelling case studies that illustrate how individuals have successfully combined visualization techniques, affirmations, gratitude, and meditation to overcome limiting beliefs and achieve their goals. Each case study highlights distinct approaches, demonstrating that there is no one-size-fits-all method; rather, success comes from personalizing these practices to align with one's unique aspirations and challenges.

One notable case study involves a young entrepreneur named Lisa, who struggled with self-doubt and a lack of focus. By incorporating daily visualization techniques into her routine, Lisa began to see herself not just as a business owner, but as a successful leader in her field. She would spend time each day vividly imagining her ideal business scenario, complete with the feelings of accomplishment and joy that accompanied it. This practice not only helped her clarify her goals but also reinforced her belief in her capabilities. Over time, Lisa noticed a shift in her mindset that allowed her to take actionable steps toward her business, ultimately leading to a flourishing startup.

Another compelling story comes from Tom, who faced significant financial challenges due to deeply ingrained limiting beliefs about money. After attending a workshop on the Law of Attraction, Tom learned about the power of daily affirmations. He began crafting affirmations that addressed his specific fears, such as "I attract abundance effortlessly" and "I am worthy of financial freedom." By repeating these affirmations each morning, Tom started to rewire his thought patterns, gradually replacing scarcity with abundance. Over several months, he reported not only an increase in his income but also a newfound sense of empowerment and confidence in his financial decisions.

Gratitude also plays a pivotal role in the manifestation process, as demonstrated by Sarah, a single mother seeking a better work-life balance. Feeling overwhelmed and frustrated, Sarah decided to implement a gratitude journal into her daily routine. Each evening, she would write down three things she was thankful for, focusing on both small victories and larger accomplishments. This practice shifted her perspective, allowing her to appreciate her current circumstances while remaining open to new opportunities. As a result, Sarah found a fulfilling job that provided the flexibility she needed, illustrating how gratitude can enhance attraction by aligning one's emotional state with the frequency of abundance.

Lastly, the integration of meditation practices has proven transformative for individuals like Mark, who struggled with anxiety and uncertainty about his career path. By committing to a daily meditation practice focused on aligning with universal laws, Mark found clarity and peace. He utilized guided meditations that emphasized manifesting his ideal career and cultivating emotional alignment. Over time, Mark experienced a profound shift in his mindset, leading him to take bolder steps in his career, including pursuing a long-desired promotion. His experience underscores the importance of emotional alignment in manifestation and the effectiveness of meditation as a tool for tuning into one's desires.

These case studies exemplify the power of integrated practices in harnessing the Law of Attraction. By combining visualization, affirmations, gratitude, and meditation, individuals can create a holistic approach that not only addresses their goals but also fosters a deeper connection to their inner selves. As illustrated through these stories, the journey of manifestation is not merely about achieving external success; it is equally about transforming one's mindset, overcoming limiting beliefs, and cultivating a life aligned with abundance.

Chapter 10: The Importance of Emotional Alignment in Manifestation

Understanding Emotional Alignment

Emotional alignment is a critical component of the manifestation process, as it directly influences our ability to attract what we desire. At its core, emotional alignment refers to the harmonious connection between our feelings, beliefs, and the outcomes we wish to achieve. When our emotions resonate with our intentions, we create a powerful energetic frequency that aligns with the universal laws of attraction. Understanding this concept is essential for anyone seeking to manifest health, wealth, and success in their lives.

To achieve emotional alignment, it is important to first identify and release any limiting beliefs that may block our path. These beliefs often stem from past experiences or societal conditioning, leading us to doubt our potential. By recognizing these limiting thoughts, we can begin to replace them with empowering affirmations that support our goals. Daily affirmations serve as a tool to reprogram our subconscious mind, reinforcing positive beliefs that align with our desired outcomes. Through consistent practice, we can shift our emotional state, paving the way for smoother manifestation.

Gratitude plays a vital role in emotional alignment as well. When we cultivate a mindset of gratitude, we shift our focus from what we lack to what we already have. This shift in perspective elevates our emotional state, making it easier to attract abundance. By expressing gratitude daily, whether through journaling, verbal acknowledgment, or meditation, we reinforce the positive emotions associated with our desires. This practice not only enhances our emotional alignment but also creates a magnetic energy that draws in the opportunities and resources we seek.

Meditation is another powerful practice for achieving emotional alignment. By quieting the mind and turning inward, we can access deeper layers of our consciousness and connect with our true desires. Through meditation, we can visualize our goals, feel the emotions associated with achieving them, and align our energy with those outcomes. Incorporating meditation into our daily routine can significantly enhance our ability to stay emotionally aligned, allowing us to navigate challenges with greater ease and focus on our aspirations.

Lastly, creating a vision board can serve as a tangible representation of our goals and desires, enhancing emotional alignment further. A vision board is not just a collection of images; it is a visual reminder of what we are working towards. When we engage with our vision board regularly, we evoke the emotions tied to our aspirations, reinforcing our commitment to manifesting them. In doing so, we create a powerful synergy between our emotional state and our goals, ultimately leading to a more successful manifestation journey. Understanding and nurturing emotional alignment is essential for anyone looking to harness the power of the universe and transform their lives.

Techniques to Achieve Emotional Alignment

Emotional alignment is a vital concept in the journey toward manifestation and personal transformation. It refers to the state of being in harmony with your emotions, thoughts, and beliefs, ensuring that they resonate with the reality you wish to create. To achieve emotional alignment, individuals must first recognize the power of their emotions and how they influence their experiences. This subchapter will explore effective techniques to attain this alignment, emphasizing practical steps that can be integrated into daily life.

Visualization techniques are one of the most powerful methods for achieving emotional alignment. By vividly imagining your desired outcomes, you create a mental image that aligns with your goals. This process not only helps clarify what you truly want but also generates positive emotions associated with those desires. To effectively visualize, find a quiet space, close your eyes, and spend a few minutes picturing your goals as if they have already been achieved. Engage all your senses in this exercise; feel the emotions of success, see the details of your dream life, and even listen to the sounds that accompany your achievements. Regularly practicing visualization can significantly elevate your emotional state and align you with the universal energies that foster attraction.

Overcoming limiting beliefs is another crucial technique for emotional alignment. Often, deeply ingrained beliefs about self-worth, success, or abundance can hinder our ability to manifest our desires. To address these limiting beliefs, begin by identifying them through self-reflection or journaling. Once recognized, challenge these beliefs by questioning their validity and replacing them with empowering affirmations. For instance, if you believe you are not deserving of success, rewrite this belief to affirm that you are worthy of abundance and prosperity. By consistently confronting and reframing these beliefs, you can shift your emotional state toward one that attracts the opportunities and outcomes you seek.

Daily affirmations also play a pivotal role in achieving emotional alignment. These positive statements help reprogram your subconscious mind, encouraging a mindset that resonates with abundance and success. To incorporate affirmations into your routine, choose statements that reflect your goals and desired emotional state. For example, repeat phrases like "I am open to receiving all the wealth the universe has to offer" or "I attract positive relationships effortlessly." Reciting these affirmations daily, particularly in the morning or before sleep, can significantly impact your emotional well-being, fostering a mindset that aligns with your aspirations.

Gratitude is another essential element in the process of emotional alignment. Expressing gratitude not only shifts your focus from lack to abundance but also elevates your emotional vibration. To harness the power of gratitude, maintain a gratitude journal where you regularly write down things you are thankful for. This practice cultivates a positive mindset, encouraging you to recognize the abundance already present in your life. As you develop a habit of gratitude, you will find it easier to align your emotions with your desires, enhancing your ability to attract what you want. Combining these techniques—visualization, overcoming limiting beliefs, affirmations, and gratitude—creates a robust foundation for emotional alignment, setting the stage for successful manifestation and transformation.

Success Stories of Emotional Transformation

The journey of emotional transformation is vital in realizing the principles of the Law of Attraction, encapsulating the profound changes individuals can experience when they align their emotions with their goals. This subchapter explores powerful success stories that illustrate how emotional shifts have led to significant manifestations in various aspects of life, including health, wealth, and personal success. By examining these narratives, readers can gain insight into practical applications of the 12 steps and how emotional alignment plays a crucial role in achieving desired outcomes.

One compelling story comes from Sarah, who struggled with chronic anxiety and self-doubt that held her back in both her career and personal life. After discovering visualization techniques, she began to create vivid mental images of her ideal self and the life she wanted to lead. By engaging in daily visualizations, Sarah gradually transformed her mindset. She replaced limiting beliefs with empowering affirmations, which allowed her to step out of her comfort zone and pursue a long-desired promotion at work. As her emotional state shifted from fear to confidence, Sarah not only achieved her career goal but also experienced a profound sense of personal fulfillment and joy.

Another inspiring example is that of James, who learned the importance of gratitude in attracting abundance. Initially, he faced financial difficulties and felt trapped in a cycle of negativity. By incorporating a daily gratitude practice into his life, he began to focus on what he had rather than what he lacked. This shift in perspective opened his eyes to new opportunities and resources around him. James started to notice small windfalls and unexpected support from friends and family, which gradually helped him stabilize his finances. His story exemplifies how emotional alignment through gratitude can enhance one's ability to attract prosperity.

Meditation practices also play a significant role in emotional transformation and alignment with universal laws. Lisa, for example, faced overwhelming stress and an inability to manifest her goals. After integrating a structured meditation routine into her daily life, she experienced a remarkable shift. Lisa discovered that through mindfulness, she could observe her thoughts and emotions without judgment, allowing her to release negative patterns. This newfound clarity and peace enabled her to focus on her aspirations, leading to successful outcomes in her career and personal relationships. Her journey highlights how meditation can serve as a powerful tool for emotional healing and alignment.

Finally, the story of Michael demonstrates the effectiveness of creating vision boards as a method of emotional transformation. Initially skeptical about the Law of Attraction, he decided to give it a try after witnessing the success of others. By crafting a vision board filled with images and words representing his goals, Michael engaged his emotions in a tangible way. This visual representation became a daily reminder of his aspirations, reinforcing his commitment to them. Over time, he noticed that as his emotional state shifted to one of excitement and anticipation, the opportunities he sought began to manifest in his life.

Michael's experience illustrates the connection between emotional alignment and the actualization of dreams through visualization techniques.

These success stories reflect the transformative power of emotional alignment in the context of the Law of Attraction. By sharing these real-life applications of the 12 steps, readers can draw inspiration and actionable insights to begin their own journeys toward manifestation and transformation. Recognizing that emotional well-being is foundational to attracting success, health, and wealth is essential in navigating the path to a fulfilling life.

Chapter 11: Success Stories: Real-Life Applications of the 12 Steps

Overview of Key Success Stories

In the journey of personal transformation and success, real-life stories serve as powerful testimonials to the effectiveness of the principles outlined in "12 Steps to Success." This subchapter, "Overview of Key Success Stories," highlights several remarkable accounts that exemplify the profound impact of manifestation techniques and the Law of Attraction. These narratives not only inspire but also provide concrete examples of how individuals have applied these principles in their lives, demonstrating that the power to create change lies within each person.

One of the most compelling success stories comes from an individual who struggled with self-doubt and limiting beliefs. Through a consistent practice of daily affirmations, she was able to rewire her internal dialogue, replacing negative thoughts with empowering statements. This shift in mindset opened doors to new opportunities in her career, leading to a promotion that she once believed was unattainable. Her experience underscores the importance of overcoming limiting beliefs and highlights how affirmations can catalyze significant changes in one's life.

Another powerful account involves a man who turned to visualization techniques after facing financial challenges. By creating a detailed vision board that depicted his goals and aspirations, he was able to clarify his intentions and stay focused on his path to success. Each image on the board served as a reminder of what he was working towards, and through diligent practice, he manifested not only financial stability but also a deeper sense of purpose. This story illustrates the effectiveness of visual tools in enhancing clarity and motivation, proving that a well-crafted vision board can be a game-changer in the manifestation process.

Gratitude also plays a pivotal role in many success stories, as evidenced by a woman who transformed her relationship with money. By adopting a daily gratitude practice, she began to recognize and appreciate the abundance in her life, shifting her focus from scarcity to plenty. This change in perspective allowed her to attract even more wealth and opportunities. Her journey emphasizes the significance of gratitude in enhancing one's ability to attract abundance and serves as a reminder that appreciation can amplify the energies of the Law of Attraction.

Lastly, the integration of meditation practices with the Law of Attraction is beautifully illustrated in the story of a young entrepreneur. Struggling with stress and overwhelm, he began a meditation routine aimed at aligning his thoughts and emotions with his goals. This practice not only improved his mental clarity but also helped him connect with the universal laws that govern manifestation. As he became more aligned with his inner self, he witnessed remarkable changes in his business, including increased clients and revenue. His experience highlights the importance of emotional alignment and spiritual practices in the manifestation journey, reinforcing that success is often a holistic endeavor that encompasses mind, body, and spirit.

These key success stories reveal the transformative power of the principles discussed in "12 Steps to Success." They serve not only as inspiration but also as practical examples of how individuals can harness the Law of Attraction and related techniques to create the lives they desire. Each story reflects the unique journey of its author, yet they collectively affirm that with intention, persistence, and the right mindset, anyone can tap into their innate potential for success and abundance.

Lessons Learned from Each Story

In the journey of manifestation and transformation, the stories shared within "12 Steps to Success" serve as powerful lessons that illuminate the path towards achieving health, wealth, and success. Each narrative encapsulates unique experiences and insights that resonate with the principles of the Law of Attraction. By examining these stories, readers can glean valuable teachings that can be applied to their own lives, enhancing their understanding of universal attraction and the practical steps involved in manifesting their desires.

One overarching lesson from these stories is the significance of visualization techniques in the manifestation process. Many individuals recount how vividly picturing their goals helped them to not only clarify their aspirations but also to summon the emotional energy necessary to attract those realities. Visualization acts as a mental rehearsal, allowing individuals to experience the feelings associated with achieving their desires, which aligns them with the vibrational frequency of abundance. Readers can incorporate this technique into their daily practices, reinforcing the connection between thought and reality.

Another key takeaway is the critical role of overcoming limiting beliefs. Numerous accounts highlight how self-doubt and negative self-talk initially hindered progress and manifested as obstacles in their journeys. By recognizing and dismantling these mental barriers, individuals reported transformative shifts that allowed them to embrace their true potential. This lesson emphasizes the importance of cultivating a mindset that supports abundance and success, encouraging readers to identify their own limiting beliefs and replace them with empowering thoughts.

Daily affirmations emerged as a powerful tool in these stories, showcasing their ability to reshape mental patterns and foster a positive outlook. Participants shared how consistently affirming their worthiness and capabilities led to significant changes in their circumstances. This practice not only reinforces self-belief but also aligns one's mental state with the energy of attraction. Readers are encouraged to develop their own affirmation routines, tailoring them to reflect personal goals and aspirations, thereby creating a strong foundation for manifesting their desires.

Gratitude also surfaces as a recurring theme in these narratives, underscoring its vital role in enhancing attraction. Many individuals found that expressing gratitude for their current circumstances, even before achieving their goals, opened the floodgates for more abundance. This practice shifts focus from lack to appreciation, creating a positive feedback loop that amplifies the energy of attraction. By integrating gratitude into their daily lives, readers can cultivate a mindset that magnetizes opportunities and fosters a deeper connection with the universal laws of attraction.

In summary, the lessons learned from these transformative stories not only provide inspiration but also offer practical guidance for those seeking to harness the power of the Law of Attraction. By embracing visualization techniques, overcoming limiting beliefs, implementing daily affirmations, and practicing gratitude, individuals can align themselves with the energy of success and abundance. Each story serves as a testament to the possibilities that await when one is committed to the journey of manifestation and transformation, empowering readers to start their own paths today.

Inspiration for Your Journey

Inspiration is a vital catalyst on your journey toward success, particularly within the framework of the 12 steps to manifestation and transformation. It serves as the fuel that ignites your ambitions and sustains your motivation through challenges. To harness this inspiration, begin by exploring the stories of individuals who have successfully navigated their paths using the principles of the Law of Attraction. These narratives not only provide real-life applications of the 12 steps but also reveal the diverse ways people have overcome obstacles and limiting beliefs to achieve their goals. By learning from their experiences, you can cultivate a mindset that embraces possibility and resilience, essential qualities for attracting health, wealth, and success.

Visualization techniques are a powerful tool for enhancing your journey. When you vividly imagine your desired outcomes, you engage your subconscious mind in the process of manifestation. Creating a mental picture of your goals helps clarify your intentions and aligns your energy with what you wish to attract. This practice can include visualizing your ideal life, career, or relationships, allowing you to feel the emotions associated with achieving these aspirations. As you incorporate visualization into your daily routine, you will find that it not only inspires you but also reinforces your belief in the Law of Attraction, laying a solid foundation for your success.

Overcoming limiting beliefs is another crucial aspect of your journey. Many individuals unknowingly hold onto negative self-perceptions that hinder their ability to manifest their desires. Recognizing and challenging these beliefs is essential to unlocking your full potential. Techniques such as journaling and introspection can help identify these barriers. Once acknowledged, you can reframe these limiting beliefs into empowering affirmations that reinforce your ability to attract abundance. By consistently affirming your worth and capability, you will gradually shift your mindset, making space for new possibilities and enhancing your overall emotional alignment with your goals.

Gratitude plays a significant role in enhancing attraction and is a key element of the manifestation process. By cultivating an attitude of gratitude, you focus on the abundance already present in your life, which attracts more positivity and success. Daily gratitude practices, whether through journaling or verbal acknowledgment, can create a powerful shift in your energy. This shift not only elevates your mood but also aligns you with the vibrations of abundance, making it easier for the universe to respond to your desires. As you incorporate gratitude into your daily life, you will find it becomes a source of inspiration, propelling you further along your journey.

Lastly, integrating meditation practices into your routine can significantly enhance your alignment with universal laws. Meditation allows you to quiet the mind, facilitating a deeper connection with your inner self and the universe. This practice helps you maintain emotional balance and clarity, essential for effective manifestation. By dedicating time to meditate, you open yourself to inspiration and guidance that can inform your actions and decisions. Creating a vision board can also complement your meditation practice by providing a tangible representation of your goals. This visual reminder keeps your aspirations at the forefront of your mind, inspiring you daily to take steps toward your desired future. Together, these practices create a harmonious cycle of inspiration, motivation, and manifestation, guiding you on your path to success.

Chapter 12: Taking Action: Your 12-Step Guide to Success

Overview of the 12 Steps

The "12 Steps to Success" framework provides a comprehensive guide for individuals seeking to harness the power of manifestation in their lives. This approach intertwines various techniques, principles, and practices that align with universal laws, aiming to help individuals achieve health, wealth, and overall success. Each step is meticulously crafted to address different aspects of the manifestation journey, ensuring that practitioners can cultivate a holistic understanding and application of the Law of Attraction.

The process begins with understanding the importance of visualization techniques for manifestation. Visualization serves as a powerful tool that allows individuals to create vivid mental images of their desires. This step emphasizes not just imagining success but feeling the emotions associated with it, thus reinforcing the belief that it is achievable. Incorporating daily practices of visualization can significantly shift one's mindset, making it easier to attract desired outcomes into reality.

Overcoming limiting beliefs is a crucial component of the 12 Steps. Many individuals unknowingly carry beliefs that hinder their potential for success. This step guides practitioners to identify and dismantle these barriers, replacing them with empowering thoughts that align with their goals. By addressing and reshaping these beliefs, individuals can create a fertile ground for abundance and prosperity, enabling them to embrace the possibilities that the universe offers.

Daily affirmations play a pivotal role in the manifestation process, acting as a constant reminder of one's intentions and desires. This step encourages the habitual practice of affirmations, which can reprogram the subconscious mind to focus on positivity and abundance. The impact of consistent affirmations not only cultivates a sense of self-belief but also enhances emotional alignment, making it easier to attract what one truly desires. When combined with gratitude practices, the effectiveness of affirmations multiplies, as gratitude opens the heart and mind to receiving more blessings.

Lastly, integrating meditation practices within the 12 Steps fosters a deeper connection with universal laws. This step highlights the importance of quieting the mind to align with higher vibrations, allowing for clearer insights and guidance. Meditation enhances one's ability to manifest by promoting emotional stability and clarity of purpose. By combining meditation with the creation of vision boards, individuals can visualize and manifest their dreams more effectively. Overall, the 12 Steps serve as a transformative guide, empowering individuals to take actionable steps toward their aspirations while embracing the principles of the Law of Attraction.

Creating Your Action Plan

Creating your action plan is an essential step in the journey toward manifesting your desires and achieving lasting transformation. This plan acts as a roadmap, guiding you through the process of aligning your thoughts, emotions, and actions with the principles of the Law of Attraction. To create an effective action plan, begin by clearly defining your goals. Consider the areas of your life you wish to improve—be it health, wealth, relationships, or personal growth. Specificity is crucial; instead of vague aspirations like "I want to be healthy," frame your goal as "I will exercise three times a week and eat more whole foods."

Once your goals are articulated, the next step is to identify the limiting beliefs that may hinder your progress. These beliefs often stem from past experiences or societal conditioning, leading to self-doubt and fear. Take time to reflect on your thoughts and feelings surrounding your goals. For instance, if you desire financial abundance but believe "money is hard to come by," acknowledge this belief and work on overcoming it. Techniques such as journaling about your beliefs, speaking to a mentor, or engaging in cognitive restructuring can be effective in shifting your mindset. Replacing negative narratives with empowering affirmations will lay a solid foundation for your action plan.

Incorporating daily affirmations is another powerful aspect of your action plan. Affirmations are positive statements that reinforce your goals and help reprogram your subconscious mind. Create a list of affirmations that resonate with your aspirations, such as "I am worthy of success" or "Abundance flows to me effortlessly." Commit to reciting these affirmations daily, ideally in front of a mirror or during meditation. This practice not only boosts your confidence but also aligns your energy with the abundance you wish to attract, creating a magnetic pull toward your goals.

Gratitude plays a pivotal role in enhancing your action plan. Cultivating an attitude of gratitude shifts your focus from what you lack to appreciating what you already have. Consider starting a gratitude journal where you write down things you're thankful for each day, which can include both small wins and larger achievements. This habit fosters a positive mindset and raises your vibrational frequency, making you more receptive to the opportunities and abundance that the universe has to offer. Remember, the more you express gratitude, the more reasons you will find to be grateful.

Finally, visualize your success regularly to reinforce your action plan. Visualization techniques help bridge the gap between your current reality and your desired outcomes by creating a mental image of success. Spend a few minutes each day in meditation, visualizing yourself achieving your goals. Engage all your senses in the process; see, hear, and feel the experience as if it is happening right now. This not only strengthens your emotional alignment with your goals but also activates the Law of Attraction, drawing your desires closer to you. By creating a structured action plan that includes clear goals, overcoming limiting beliefs, daily affirmations, gratitude practices, and visualization, you set yourself on a transformative path toward success and abundance.

Commitment to Your Manifestation Journey

Embarking on a manifestation journey requires a steadfast commitment to your goals and desires. In the realm of the Law of Attraction, this commitment serves as the foundation for all subsequent actions and beliefs. It requires a clear understanding of what you truly want, paired with the determination to pursue those desires relentlessly. Your commitment acts as a guiding light, illuminating the path even when challenges arise. As you progress through the 12 steps outlined in this book, maintaining focus on your intentions will empower you to navigate obstacles and align with the abundance you seek.

Visualization techniques play a crucial role in reinforcing your commitment. By regularly visualizing your desired outcomes, you create a mental image that strengthens your belief in their attainment. This practice not only enhances your emotional connection to your goals but also serves to rewire your subconscious mind. The more vividly you can imagine your success, the more likely it is that you will attract opportunities that align with your vision. Incorporating visualization into your daily routine can transform your commitment from a fleeting thought into a powerful driving force that propels you forward.

Overcoming limiting beliefs is another essential aspect of commitment in the manifestation process. Many individuals unknowingly carry subconscious beliefs that hinder their progress. These beliefs can manifest as self-doubt or a sense of unworthiness, which can obstruct the flow of abundance. By committing to identifying and challenging these limiting beliefs, you can pave the way for a healthier mindset. Techniques such as journaling and affirmations can be instrumental in this process, allowing you to confront and replace negative thought patterns with empowering beliefs that support your journey.

Daily affirmations are a vital tool for reinforcing your commitment to manifestation. By routinely expressing positive statements about your goals and capabilities, you cultivate a mindset that is conducive to attracting abundance. Affirmations act as a reminder of your intentions, helping to keep your focus sharp and your motivation high. The simple act of verbalizing your desires empowers you to take ownership of your journey, making it easier to remain committed even during challenging times. Incorporating affirmations into your morning routine can set a positive tone for the day ahead, keeping your dreams at the forefront of your mind.

Gratitude is another powerful element that enhances your commitment to manifestation. Acknowledging and appreciating what you currently have creates an energetic shift that aligns you with the frequency of abundance. This practice not only grounds you in the present but also opens your heart to new possibilities. When you express gratitude, you reinforce your commitment to attracting more positive experiences into your life. By integrating gratitude into your daily practices—whether through journaling, meditation, or simple reflection—you align yourself with the universal laws of attraction, further solidifying your path to success.

Don't miss out!

Visit the website below and you can sign up to receive emails whenever Digby R. Kerr publishes a new book. There's no charge and no obligation.

https://books2read.com/r/B-A-BKGHC-CCDYE

BOOKS 2 READ

Connecting independent readers to independent writers.

Also by Digby R. Kerr

The Ripple Effect

The Ripple Effect: "A Fable About Embracing Change and Thriving in Uncertainty"

The Ripple Effect: "A Fable About Embracing Change and Thriving in Uncertainty"

Standalone

The Universal Code: Unlocking the Secrets of Happiness, Wealth, and Health

Mastering LinkedIn: A Comprehensive Guide to Building Your Profile, Growing Your Audience, and Leveraging Business Opportunities

The Universal Code: Unlocking the Secrets of Happiness, Wealth, and Health

Cross-Border Trade Compliance: Navigating the Global Marketplace

Report on Trends and Challenges in Logistics Hiring

"12 Steps to Success: Real-Life Stories of Manifestation and Transformation"

Watch for more at https://www.linkedin.com/in/digbyrkerr/.

About the Author

About the Author

Digby R. Kerr Founder, President & CEO of Logistics Consulting, Inc.Partnered with & Powered by the R+R Group, Family of Companies

Digby R. Kerr is a distinguished global logistics expert and entrepreneur whose profound journey has been marked by both triumphs and trials. From his early life in Borehamwood, London, to his rise in New York and beyond, Digby's path has been a testament to the transformative power of universal principles and personal resilience.

A lifelong learner and seeker of wisdom, Digby has delved deeply into the mysteries of happiness, wealth, and health, drawing from a wealth of knowledge, personal experiences, and interactions with leading experts in psychology, neuroscience, and spirituality. His insights into universal thought and processes have shaped his approach to life and business, guiding him through challenges and leading him to a life of abundance and fulfillment.

In his book, **"Unlocking the Secrets of Happiness, Wealth, and Health,"** Digby shares the transformative teachings and practical strategies that have profoundly impacted his life. By revealing the principles that have helped him navigate his own journey, he offers readers a roadmap to unlock their own potential and achieve their desires. His story is not just one of success but of deep personal transformation, illustrating how understanding and applying universal principles can lead to extraordinary results.

Connect with Digby R. Kerr LinkedIn: Digby R. KerrEmail: DKNYPublishing@icloud.comWebsite: DKNY Publishing

Discover more about Digby's journey, his groundbreaking work, and how his publishing company supports rising star authors with expert guidance and professional support.

Read more at https://www.linkedin.com/in/digbyrkerr/.

9 798822 667465